MW00984877

Carol Ann Duffy lives in Manchester, where she is Professor and Creative Director of the Writing School at Manchester Metropolitan University. She was Poet Laureate from 2009 to 2019. She has written for both children and adults, and her poetry has received many awards, including the Signal Prize for Children's Verse, the Whitbread, Forward and T.S. Eliot Prizes, and the Lannan and E.M. Forster Prizes in America. In 2011 *The Bees* won the Costa Poetry Award, and in 2012 she won the PEN Pinter Prize. She was appointed DBE in 2015. In 2021, she was awarded the Golden Wreath, an international award for lifetime achievement in poetry.

Also by Carol Ann Duffy in Picador

Standing Female Nude
Selling Manhattan
The Other Country
Mean Time
The World's Wife
Feminine Gospels
New Selected Poems
Rapture
Mrs Scrooge
Love Poems
Another Night Before Christmas
The Bees
The Christmas Truce
Wenceslas
Bethlehem
Ritual Lighting
Dorothy Wordsworth's Christmas Birthday
Collected Poems
The Wren-Boys
The King of Christmas
Pablo Picasso's Noël
Frost Fair
Sincerity
Christmas Poems
Advent Street
Love
Elegies
Nature
Politics
Christmas Eve at The Moon Under Water

AS EDITOR

Hand in Hand
Answering Back
To the Moon
Off the Shelf
Empty Nest

Earth Prayers

Encounters in Poetry with the Natural World

Edited by

CAROL ANN DUFFY

PICADOR

First published 2024 by Picador
an imprint of Pan Macmillan
The Smithson, 6 Briset Street, London EC1M 5NR
EU representative: Macmillan Publishers Ireland Ltd, 1st Floor,
The Liffey Trust Centre, 117–126 Sheriff Street Upper,
Dublin 1, D01 YC43
Associated companies throughout the world
www.panmacmillan.com

ISBN 978-1-0350-4814-4

The permissions acknowledgements on pp. 141–6
constitute an extension of this copyright page.

1 3 5 7 9 8 6 4 2

A CIP catalogue record for this book is available from the British Library.

Printed and bound by CPI Group (UK) Ltd, Croydon, CR0 4YY

Contents

so that my mind would be one selving or pitch of a great universal mind, working in other minds too besides mine, and even in all other things, according to their natures and powers.

GERARD MANLEY HOPKINS

Foreword

'We didn't travel all this way / to break your hearts. We came to ask if you might heal the world.' John Glenday's lines in the opening poem here could apply to the remarkable time-travel of long dead poets' poems. John Clare published 'The Mores' in 1820: between 1809 and then, the English Acts of Enclosure allowed landowners to fence, bar, chop, burn, drain, re-route and parcel up the landscape of Clare's youth. His suffering and mental distress at this were and are still mirrored in indigenous peoples across the globe. 'Long live the weeds and the wilderness yet', wrote the poet-priest Gerard Manley Hopkins in 1881; a blessing and apprehension answered by Paula Meehan in 'Death of a Field', 2009. And, for many, the collective sorrow at the mindless felling of the Sycamore Gap tree in 2023 is already articulated by Charlotte Mew in her 1920s poem, 'The Trees Are Down'.

We are in the age of anthropogenic climate breakdown, possibly the Age of Grief. Nearly sixty per cent of the world's population lives in cities and by 2050 this number is expected to double to nearly nine billion inhabitants – seven in ten of us. Few will ever wander lonely as clouds and the hand of the poet can no longer write the Nature poem. 'My mind's indicted by all I've taken', writes A. R. Ammons (1926–2001) in 'Plunder' on doing just that. Yet the poems of the past illuminate, for writers and readers, what we have lost and are losing, and poets like John Clare are the ancestors of Ecopoetry. There is no poem without an earlier poem.

In 2023, during COP28 in Dubai, an open letter from Scientist Rebellion (fifteen hundred scientists and academics) spoke of their terror at the lack of impact of their published scientific evidence on the Climate Catastrophe. Their words, they declared, are not being heard or acted upon. 'There is no Planet B', the T-shirts read, going round and round in the tumble dryers. So what can the words of poems achieve? The poems here are all hallmarked with the humility required to write a true poem at all. Not with a sense of dominion over the earth and over every swimming, flying, creeping thing, but with gratitude, equality and, rightly, remorse. The anger looks at the human. Sometimes there are moments of epiphany, as rendered by Hopkins or Heaney; or there are hot flashes of shame from Denise Levertov or D. H. Lawrence; or despair from Lucille Clifton and Stevie Smith. Queer, political, celebratory or elegiac, they are moments in language to pause and allow ourselves to see differently. From their diverse years, they seek readers. The future is here and these are its prayers.

Carol Ann Duffy

Earth Prayers

The Walkers

As soon as we had died, we decided to walk home.
A white tatterflag marked where each journey began.
It was a slow business, so much water to be crossed,
so many dirt roads followed. We walked together but alone.

You must understand – we can never be passengers any more.
Even the smallest children had to make their own way
to their graves, through acres and acres of sunflowers,
somehow no longer pretty. A soldier cradled a cigarette, a teddy bear

and his gun. He didn't see us pass, our light was far too thin.
We skirted villages and cities, traced the meanderings of rivers.
But beyond it all, the voices of our loved ones called
so we flowed through borders like the wind through railings

and when impassable mountains marked the way,
soared above their peaks like flocks of cloud, like shoals of rain.
In time the fields and woods grew weary and the sea began –
you could tell we were home by the way our shadows leaned.

We gathered like craneflies in the windowlight of familiar rooms,
grieving for all the things we could never hold again.
Forgive us for coming back. We didn't travel all this way
to break your hearts. We came to ask if you might heal the world.

JOHN GLENDAY

Poem

The earth said
remember me.
The earth said
don't let go,

said it one day
when I was
accidentally
listening, I

heard it, I felt it
like temperature,
all said in a
whisper – build to-

morrow, make right be-
fall, you are not
free, other scenes
are not taking

place, time is not filled,
time is not late, there is
a thing the emptiness
needs as you need

emptiness, it
shrinks from light again &
again, although all things
are present, a

fact a day a
bird that warps the
arithmetic of per-
fection with its

arc, passing again &
again in the evening
air, in the pre-
vailing wind, making no

mistake – yr in-
difference is yr
principal beauty
the mind says all the

time – I hear it – I
hear it every-
where. The earth
said remember

me. I am the
earth, it said. Re-
member me.

JORIE GRAHAM

The Snow Man

One must have a mind of winter
To regard the frost and the boughs
Of the pine-trees crusted with snow;

And have been cold a long time
To behold the junipers shagged with ice,
The spruces rough in the distant glitter

Of the January sun; and not to think
Of any misery in the sound of the wind,
In the sound of a few leaves,

Which is the sound of the land
Full of the same wind
That is blowing in the same bare place

For the listener, who listens in the snow,
And, nothing himself, beholds
Nothing that is not there and the nothing that is.

WALLACE STEVENS

Walking Past a Rose This June Morning

is my heart a rose?   how unspeakable
is my heart a rose?   how unspeakable
is my heart folded to dismantle?   how unspeakable
is a rose folded in its nerves?   how unspeakable
is my heart secretly overhanging us?   pause
is there a new world   known only to breathing?
now inhale what I remember.   pause.   how unbreathable

this is my heart out.   how unspeakable
this is my risen skin.   how unthinkable
this is my tense touch-sensitive heart
this is its mass made springy by the rain
this loosening compression of hope.   how unworkable
is an invisible ray lighting up your lungs?   how invisible?
is it a weightless rapture?   pause.   how weightless?

now trace a breath-map in the air.   how invisible?
is a rose a turning cylinder of senses?   how unspeakable
is this the ghost of the heart, the actual
the inmost deceleration of its thought?   how unspeakable
is everything still speeding around us?   pause
is my heart the centre?   how unbearable
is the rain a halo?   how unbearable

ALICE OSWALD

Heirloom

She gave me childhood's flowers,
Heather and wild thyme,
Eyebright and tormentil,
Lichen's mealy cup
Dry on wind-scored stone,
The corbies on the rock,
The rowan by the burn.

Sea-marvels a child beheld
Out in the fisherman's boat,
Fringed pulsing violet
Medusa, sea-gooseberries,
Starfish on the sea-floor,
Cowries and rainbow-shells
From pools on a rocky shore.

Gave me her memories,
But kept her last treasure:
'When I was a lass', she said,
'Sitting among the heather,
Suddenly I saw
That all the moor was alive!
I have told no one before'.

That was my mother's tale.
Seventy years had gone
Since she saw the living skein
Of which the world is woven,
And having seen, knew all;
Through long indifferent years
Treasuring the priceless pearl.

KATHLEEN RAINE

the earth is a living thing

is a black shambling bear
ruffling its wild back and tossing
mountains into the sea

is a black hawk circling
the burying ground circling the bones
picked clean and discarded

is a fish black blind in the belly of water
is a diamond blind in the black belly of coal

is a black and living thing
is a favorite child
of the universe
feel her rolling her hand
in its kinky hair
feel her brushing it clean

LUCILLE CLIFTON

Daisies

Go ahead: say what you're thinking. The garden
is not the real world. Machines
are the real world. Say frankly what any fool
could read in your face: it makes sense
to avoid us, to resist
nostalgia. It is
not modern enough, the sound the wind makes
stirring a meadow of daisies: the mind
cannot shine following it. And the mind
wants to shine, plainly, as
machines shine, and not
grow deep, as, for example, roots. It is very touching,
all the same, to see you cautiously
approaching the meadow's border in early morning,
when no one could possibly
be watching you. The longer you stand at the edge,
the more nervous you seem. No one wants to hear
impressions of the natural world: you will be
laughed at again; scorn will be piled on you.
As for what you're actually
hearing this morning: think twice
before you tell anyone what was said in this field
and by whom.

LOUISE GLUCK

I Kicked a Mushroom

and then I felt bad.
And not just some cute toadstool or gnome's bed
but a fruiting body of brain-coloured discs
as wide as a manhole cover or bin lid,
a raft of silky caps basted in light rain
stemming from one root as thick as a wrist,
anchored in deep earth, like a rope on a beach.
One jab with a spade would have done the job,
then a pitchfork to hoik it over the hedge,
but I stuck in the boot then walked away
with its white meat caught in my tongue and lace.
All night it lies on the lawn inside out,
its tripes and corals turned to the stars,
gills in the air, showing the gods what I am.

SIMON ARMITAGE

Moss-Gathering

To loosen with all ten fingers held wide and limber
And lift up a patch, dark-green, the kind for lining cemetery
baskets,
Thick and cushiony, like an old-fashioned doormat,
The crumbling small hollow sticks on the underside mixed with
roots,
And wintergreen berries and leaves still stuck to the top, –
That was moss-gathering.
But something always went out of me when I dug loose those
carpets
Of green, or plunged to my elbows in the spongy yellowish moss of
the marshes:
And afterwards I always felt mean, jogging back over the logging
road,
As if I had broken the natural order of things in that swampland;
Disturbed some rhythm, old and of vast importance,
By pulling off flesh from the living planet;
As if I had committed, against the whole scheme of life, a
desecration.

THEODORE ROETHKE

The Blossom

A May morning.
Light starting in the sky.

I have come here
after a long night.
Its senses of loss.
Its unrelenting memories of happiness.

The blossom on the apple tree is still in shadow,
its petals half-white and filled with water at the core,
in which the freshness and secrecy of dawn are stored
even in the dark.

How much longer
will I see girlhood in my daughter?

In other seasons
I knew every leaf on this tree.
Now I stand here
almost without seeing them

and so lost in grief
I hardly notice what is happening
as the light increases and the blossom speaks,
and turns to me
with blonde hair and my eyebrows and says –

imagine if I stayed here,
even for the sake of your love,
what would happen to the summer?
To the fruit?

Then holds out a dawn-soaked hand to me,
whose fingers I counted at birth
years ago.

And touches mine for the last time.

And falls to earth.

EAVAN BOLAND

from Jubilate Agno

For the doubling of flowers is the improvement of the gardener's
talent.
For the flowers are great blessings.
For the Lord made a Nosegay in the meadow with his disciples and
preached upon the lily.
For the angels of God took it out of his hand and carried it to the
Height.
For a man cannot have public spirit, who is void of private
benevolence.
For there is no Height in which there are not flowers.
For flowers have great virtues for all the senses.
For the flower glorifies God and the root parries the adversary.
For the flowers have their angels even the words of God's Creation.
For the warp and woof of flowers are worked by perpetual moving
spirits.
For flowers are good both for the living and the dead.
For there is a language of flowers.
For there is a sound reasoning upon all flowers.
For elegant phrases are nothing but flowers.
For flowers are peculiarly the poetry of Christ.
For flowers are medicinal.
For flowers are musical in ocular harmony.
For the right names of flowers are yet in heaven. God make
gardeners better nomenclators.
For the Poorman's nosegay is an introduction to a Prince.

CHRISTOPHER SMART

Flowers

I have never learnt the names of flowers.
From beginning, my world has been a place
Of pot-holed streets where thick, sluggish gutters race
In slow time, away from garbage heaps and sewers
Past blanched old houses around which cowers
Stagnant earth. There, scarce green things grew to chase
The dull-grey squalor of sick dust; no trace
Of plant save few sparse weeds; just these, no flowers.

One day they cleared a space and made a park
There in the city's slums; and suddenly
Came stark glory like lightning in the dark,
While perfume and bright petals thundered slowly.
I learnt no names, but hue, shape and scent mark
My mind, even now, with symbols holy.

DENNIS CRAIG

A Lesson in Botany

Consider it: in the mountains
of Malaya, on the mammoth grape:
the masterpiece, a 24-pound
flower, its diameter
28 inches in full bloom.
A triumph! Leafless, asepalous,
rootless and stemless: pure flower.

Its adhesive seeds grow
tendrils into the Tetrastigma
vine. It takes nine months to open
fully and stays open seven days.
It has five petals, reddish
brown and often mottled. All
its organs are dead-centre
in a blood-coloured, lidded cup.

Consider, furthermore, its smell,
which is precisely that of
twenty-four fully opened
pounds of rotting meat; the method
of its pollination: carrion-
eating flies; and of its seed
dissemination: fruit rats.

Sir Thomas Stamford Raffles,
the man who planted the Union
Jack on Singapore, has given it
its name: it is *Rafflesia*
arnoldi. This, of course,
is history. *Rafflesia*
arnoldi by any other
name would be *Rafflesia*
arnoldi as we know it and
the largest flower in the natural world.

ROBERT BRINGHURST

Daffodils

(Speculation on Future Blackness)

It's time to write about daffodils
again to hear

a different sound
from the word

daffodil

Imagine daffodils in the corner
of a sound system

in Clapham
Can't you?

Well you must
try to imagine daffodils

in the hands of a black family
on a black walk

in spring

JASON ALLEN-PAISANT

The Spirit of the Place

Mist like evaporating stone
smudges the bracken. Not much further now.
Below on the other side of the village
Windermere tilts its pewter face
over towards me as I move downhill.
I've walked my boots clean in gravelly streams;
picking twigs of glittering holly
to take home I've lacerated my fingers
(it serves me right: holly belongs on trees).
Now as the early dusk descends behind me
dogs in the kennels above Nook Lane
are barking, growling, hysterical at something;
and from the housing estate below
a deep mad voice bellows 'Wordsworth! Wordsworth!'

FLEUR ADCOCK

(O sweet spontaneous)

O sweet spontaneous
earth how often have
the
doting
          fingers of
prurient philosophers pinched
and
poked

thee
,has the naughty thumb
of science prodded
thy

     beauty   how
often have religions taken
thee upon their scraggy knees
squeezing and

buffeting thee that thou mightest conceive
gods
      (but
true

to the incomparable
couch of death thy
rhythmic
lover

          thou answerest

them only with

                    spring)

E.E. CUMMINGS

Mississippi Gardens

slaves, she answers, as I sink
my fingers beneath the roots.

the knees of that blue housedress are threadbare.
she wears it on Tuesdays and Fridays when we tend the flowers.

pullin' weeds ain't a time for talk, she chides.
I watch her uproot the creeping charlie.

the fragrant blossoms we protect, hug our whole house.
sweet peas were my choice.

we rarely buy those things for sale in the gardening aisle.
don't make sense to work the earth and not feel it.

I wanted those thick cotton gloves, but they stayed on the shelf.
you gotta learn the difference between dirt and soil.

sometime I notice how the ground changes.

denser, darker, moister, a little more red in some places.

in social studies class I learned about crop rotation

and how it keeps the land fertile.

Mama, what did they used to grow here?

STEPHANIE PRUITT

Grass

Pile the bodies high at Austerlitz and Waterloo.
Shovel them under and let me work—
    I am the grass; I cover all.

And pile them high at Gettysburg
And pile them high at Ypres and Verdun.
Shovel them under and let me work.
Two years, ten years, and passengers ask the conductor:
        What place is this?
        Where are we now?

        I am the grass.
        Let me work.

CARL SANDBURG

surely i am able to write poems

surely i am able to write poems
celebrating grass and how the blue
in the sky can flow green or red
and the waters lean against the
chesapeake shore like a familiar,
poems about nature and landscape
surely   but whenever i begin
'the trees wave their knotted branches
and . . .'   why
is there under that poem always
an other poem?

LUCILLE CLIFTON

Pineapple

With *yayama*
fruit of the Antilles,
we welcomed you
to our shores,
not knowing in
your language
'house warming'
meant 'to take
possession of'
and 'host'
could so easily
turn hostage.

Oblivious
of irony,
you now claim
our symbol
of hospitality
as your own,
never suspecting
the retribution
incarnate
in that sweet
flesh.

So you
plant pineapples
arrayed in fields
like battalions
not knowing
each headdress
of spikes
is slanted
to harness
the sun's
explosions

and store them
within
the fruit's
thick skin
on which
– unless
you can peel
them off quick –
pineal eyes
watch and
wait,
counting
down.

OLIVE SENIOR

I Saw in Louisiana a Live-Oak Growing

I saw in Louisiana a live-oak growing,
All alone stood it and the moss hung down from the branches,
Without any companion it grew there uttering joyous leaves of dark
green,
And its look, rude, unbending, lusty, made me think of myself,
But I wonder'd how it could utter joyous leaves standing alone there
without its friend near, for I knew I could not,
And I broke off a twig with a certain number of leaves upon
it, and twined it round a little moss,
And brought it away, and I have placed it in sight in my room,
It is not needed to remind me as of my own dear friends,
(For I believe lately I think of little else than of them,)
Yet it remains to me a curious token, it makes me think of manly
love;
For all that, and though the live-oak glistens there in Louisiana
solitary in a wide flat space,
Uttering joyous leaves all its life without a friend a lover, near,
I know very well I could not.

WALT WHITMAN

Dryad

I remember her covered in snow in a field
where each dead stalk of wildflower was thick
with frost. The sky was pink in the hawthorns,

the day held on the light-edge of breaking.
A woman carved from the bole of an oak,
her feet (if she had any) buried in the winter's

shedding weight. Whoever had turned her
from the tree had given her an orb
which she held in both hands, close to the gentle

curve of her face. And she stood there
by the half-rotten stile off Broad Lane,
head bowed, as though waiting to greet us

and offer the frozen circumference of a new
world. Years ago, our school had planted
the woods behind her, when I was eight or nine,

and now each tree ages alongside us.
Every time I go back, I see a part
of my life laid out, still growing in a field

by the old village. I used to come here
often, at eighteen or so, with men at night
and it was strange to pass her as we stumbled

in the undergrowth and into the woods
like deer plummeting through the wet branches.
And I think now of all the men forced outside

after clearing-out, into the dark spaces of towns,
how they walk in vigil to woodlands and old
estates, to the smell of the day settling. Once,

I came here with a man whose whole body
was muscled, as though he too had been carved
from a single trunk of wood. I pretended

all the time to be a man like him,
answering each lie in a deep, alien voice.
I think I was afraid he would kill me,

and walked a few steps ahead, hearing
him moving through the sodden grass,
pulling his feet from the bramble-vines.

We passed the woman without comment,
though she stood there in her cloak of wood,
the globe held in the lathed green of her hands.

Here was so unlike the places other people went,
a place without doors or walls or rooms.
The black heavy-leafed branches pulled back

like a curtain and inside a dark chamber
of the wood, guarded, and made safe.
The bed was the bed of all the plants

and trees, and we could share it. And then
the kneeling down in front of him, keeping
my secrets still in the folds of night, trying

not to shake in the cold, and the damp floor
seeping up. I remember the cold water
spreading in the capillaries of my jeans.

As I looked up, the sky hidden under a rain
of leaves, each tree stood over me
in perfect symmetry with his body.

Each was like a man with his head bent,
each watching and moving and making slow
laboured sighs. I came back often,

year on year, kneeling and being knelt for
in acts of secret worship, and now
each woodland smells quietly of sex,

not only when the air is thick with it,
but in winter too when the strains
are grounded and held against the earth,

and each time I half-expect
to meet someone among the trees
or inside the empty skeleton

of the rhododendron, and I wonder if I have ruined
these places for myself, if I have brought
each secret to them and weighed the trees

with things I can no longer bear. But then
what is a tree, or a plant, if not an act
of kneeling to the earth, a way of bidding

the water to move, of taking in the mouth
the inner part of the world and coaxing it out.
Not just the aching leaf-buds

in spring, the cloud of pollen, or in autumn
the children knocking branches for the shower
of seed, but the people who kneel in the woods

at night, the woman waiting by the gate, offering
to each visitor a small portion of the world
in which they might work for the life of it.

SEAN HEWITT

Alone in the Woods

Alone in the woods I felt
The bitter hostility of the sky and the trees
Nature has taught her creatures to hate
Man that fusses and fumes
Unquiet man
As the sap rises in the trees
As the sap paints the trees a violent green
So rises the wrath of Nature's creatures
At man
So paints the face of Nature a violent green.
Nature is sick at man
Sick at his fuss and fume
Sick at his agonies
Sick at his gaudy mind
That drives his body
Ever more quickly
More and more
In the wrong direction.

STEVIE SMITH

The Trees are Down

– and he cried with a loud voice:
Hurt not the earth, neither the sea, nor the trees –
(Revelation)

They are cutting down the great plane-trees at the end of the gardens.
For days there has been the grate of the saw, the swish of the branches as they fall,
The crash of trunks, the rustle of trodden leaves,
With the 'Whoops' and the 'Whoas', the loud common talk, the loud common laughs of the men, above it all.

I remember one evening of a long past Spring
Turning in at a gate, getting out of a cart, and finding a large dead rat in the mud of the drive.
I remember thinking, alive or dead, a rat was a god-forsaken thing,
But at least, in May, that even a rat should be alive.

The week's work here is as good as done. There is just one bough
On the roped bole, in the fine grey rain,
Green and high
And lonely against the sky.
(Down now! –)
And but for that,
If an old dead rat
Did once, for a moment, unmake the Spring, I might never have thought of him again.

It is not for a moment the Spring is unmade to-day;
These were great trees, it was in them from root to stem:
When the men with the 'Whoops' and the 'Whoas' have carted the whole of the whispering loveliness away
Half the Spring, for me, will have gone with them.

It is going now, and my heart has been struck with the hearts of
  the planes;
Half my life it has beat with these, in the sun, in the rains,
    In the March wind, the May breeze,
In the great gales that came over to them across the roofs from the
  great seas.
    There was only a quiet rain when they were dying;
    They must have heard the sparrows flying,
And the small creeping creatures in the earth where they were
  lying –
    But I, all day I heard an angel crying:
      'Hurt not the trees.'

CHARLOTTE MEW

Hawthorn

I like it when memories aren't pinned
haughtily to words, but come to find
them, slowly on the bridge
of a warm breeze filled emptily
with blackbird songs, a robin
twisting its invisible screw
and a more piercing song
I can't yet name, and beside it a scent
that belongs at the slow start
of another summer, alive
and pungent and unattached
then to the off-white flowers
a little distance off from this bench
and the name, the name.

ZAFFAR KUNIAL

Song

A rowan like a lipsticked girl
Between the by-road and the main road
Alder trees at a wet and dripping distance
Stand off among the rushes.

These are the mud-flowers of dialect
And the immortelles of perfect pitch
And that moment when the bird sings very close
To the music of what happens.

SEAMUS HEANEY

Swifts

Spring comes little, a little. All April it rains.
The new leaves stick in their fists; new ferns, still fiddleheads.
But one day the swifts are back. Face to the sun like a child
You shout, 'The swifts are back!'

Sure enough, bolt nocks bow to carry one sky-scyther
Two hundred miles an hour across fullblown windfields.
Swereee, swereee. Another. And another.
It's the cut air falling in shrieks on our chimneys and roofs.

The next day, a fleet of high crosses cruises in ether.
These are the air pilgrims, pilots of air rivers.
But a shift of wing and they're earth-skimmers, daggers
Skilful in guiding the throw of themselves away from themselves.

Quick flutter, a scimitar upsweep, out of danger of touch, for
Earth is forbidden to them, water's forbidden to them,
All air and fire, little owlish ascetics, they outfly storms,
They rush to the pillars of altitude, the thermal fountains.

Here is a legend of swifts, a parable –
When the Great Raven bent over earth to create the birds,
The swifts were ungrateful. They were small muddy things
Like shoes, with long legs and short wings,

So they took themselves off to the mountains to sulk.
And they stayed there. 'Well,' said the Raven, after years of this,
'I will give you the sky, you can have the whole sky
On condition that you give up rest.'

'Yes, yes,' screamed the swifts. 'We abhor rest.
We detest the filth of growth, the sweat of sleep,
Soft nests in the wet fields, slimehold of worms.
Let us be free, be air!'

So the Raven took their legs and bound them into their bodies.
He bent their wings like boomerangs, honed them like knives.
He streamlined their feathers and stripped them of velvet.
Then he released them, *Never to Return*

Inscribed on their feet and wings. And so
We have swifts, though in reality, not parables but
Bolts in the world's need: swift
Swifts, not in punishment, not in ecstasy, simply

Sleepers over oceans in the mill of the world's breathing.
The grace to say that they live in another firmament.
A way to say the miracle will not occur,
And watch the miracle.

ANNE STEVENSON

24.6.16

Red kites, native to Turkey, Morocco, and parts of Europe, were declared 'vermin' by the English crown and hunted nearly to extinction. They were successfully reintroduced to the UK in 1989.

No red kites over the field this morning.
However hard I looked, I could not find

a single cresting pair, their high crosses
invisible – as if unpitched from the grass.

No dry swoop, no sounding. No clatter from
morning's fed sparrows rising in alarm,

no hare's carcass eaten behind our wall,
nothing astir. No courting on the fell

in curious patterns, no stumbling display
of swift shadows bending above the Wye.

No haunt. No song. Only the heaven's blue
graceless fire, and then as a ghost pursued

across a moor, the hunting-horn's burly
cry
crucify, crucify, crucify.

THEOPHILUS KWEK

Peregrines

Soon they will kill the falcons that breed in the quarry
(it's only a matter of time: raptors need space
and, in these parts, space equals money);

but now, for a season, they fly low over the fields
and the thin paths that run to the woods
at Gillingshill,

the children calling out on Sunday walks
to stop and look
                                    and all of us
pausing to turn in our tracks while the mortgaged land

falls silent for miles around, the village below us
empty and grey as the vault where its money sleeps,
and the moment so close to sweet, while we stand and wait

for the flicker of sky in our bones
that is almost flight.

JOHN BURNSIDE

Eagle Owl

It sits in a yew's high branches,
the afternoon sun
warming its blazoned breast.

It has feasted on sparrow and pigeon.
It snoozes like a magistrate
after the morning session.

A small crowd gathers,
necks craned backwards
as if awaiting a judgement.

The rumour goes round-
a woman was swooped on
powdering her nose

as she crossed
the cathedral precinct at dusk-
it ought to be shot.

No one knows where it comes from.
Escaped from a zoo,
one man suggests.

Someone else says
it's from the forests of Siberia
blown off-course in a storm.

For months its whooo-whooo
has echoed at nights
round buttress and boss.

I think it's Athena
come down to earth
this mild winter

to see if men
have grown any wiser:
elated at first

(she's not getting any younger)
to find she could still squeeze
into her feathery dress –

then suddenly feeling
too old, tired and discouraged
to make the long flight back.

VICKI FEAVER

Brood

At sixteen, I did a day's work
on an egg farm.
A tin shed the size of a hangar.

Inside its oven dark
two thousand stacked cages,
engines of clatter and squawk.

My job, to shine a torch
through the bars for the dead hens
then pack them tight into a bin-bag.

All the time my mind chanting:
there's only one hen, just one
ruined hen repeated over and over.

In this way I soothed the sight
of all that caged battery,
their feathers stripped to stems,

their patches of scrotum skin,
their bodies held
in the dead hands of their wings.

But what kept me awake
that hot night in my box room,
as I listened to the brook outside

chew on its stones and the fox's
human scream, was how
those thousand-thousand birds

had watched me. And really
it was me repeated over and over,
set in the amber of their eyes.

Me, the frightened boy in jeans
stiff with chicken shit, carrying
a bin-bag full of small movement.

A foot that opened. An eyelid
that unshelled its blind nut.
A beak mouthing a word.

MARK PAJAK

Wild Swans

I looked in my heart while the wild swans went over,
And what did I see I had not seen before?
Only a question less or a question more;
Nothing to match the flight of wild birds flying.
Tiresome heart, forever living and dying,
House without air, I leave you and lock your door.
Wild swans, come over the town, come over
The town again, trailing your legs and crying!

EDNA ST VINCENT MILLAY

The Blackbird of Spitalfields

Four a.m. undone. No lock-ins, no vans
about their rounds, no running gangs,
just phrase on phrase of traffic heading north,
and up above the maze of roofs, a blackbird's flute,
unable to distinguish night from day.
Is it light or land that has him sing,
or fuss for unreached company? And still,
for all his thirds and major fifths,
his song not song, but simple call and speech.
Nothing sings together on this earth but us.

MATTHEW HOLLIS

Wings Over Scotland

Glenogil Estate: poisoned buzzard (Carbofuran).
No prosecution.
Millden Estate: poisoned buzzard (Alphachloralose).
No prosecution.
Millden Estate: poisoned golden eagle 'Alma' (Carbofuran).
No prosecution.
Glenogil Estate: poisoned white-tailed eagle '89' (Carbofuran).
No prosecution.
'Nr Noranside': poisoned red kite (Carbofuran).
No prosecution.
Glenogil Estate: poisoned buzzard (Chloralose).
No prosecution.
Glenogil Estate: poisoned pigeon bait (Carbofuran).
No prosecution.
Millden Estate: shot buzzard.
No prosecution.
Rottal & Tarabuckle Estate: dead kestrel
inside crow cage trap.
No prosecution.
'Nr Bridgend': remains of buzzard
found under a rock. Suspicious death.
'Nr Noranside': remains of buzzard
found beside pheasant pen. Suspicious death.
Millden Estate: satellite-tagged golden eagle
caught in spring trap, then apparently uplifted
overnight and dumped on Deeside.
No prosecution.
Glen Esk: Disappearance of sat-tagged red kite.
No other transmissions or sightings of bird.

KATHLEEN JAMIE

Midwinter

And crow
is squawking at 6.00 am
in the velveteen black
of a winter morning:
I have already had a cold
morning shower of rain
and fed my offspring
a diet of worms and wet slugs.
Meet the sun before it rises;
master your morning.
Grab that wooden spoon
and stir that gruel
for your family's breakfast.
Master your day,
you lazy human bastard.

ROGER ROBINSON

Parliament

Then in the writers' wood
every bird with a name in the world
crowded the leafless trees,
took its turn to whistle or croak.
An owl grieved in an oak.
A magpie mocked. A rook
cursed from a sycamore.
The cormorant spoke:
Stinking seas
below ill winds. Nothing swims.
A vast plastic soup, thousand miles
wide as long, of petroleum crap.

A bird of paradise wept in a willow.
The jewel of a hummingbird shrilled
on the air.
A stork shawled itself like a widow.
The gull said:
Where coral was red, now white, dead
under stunned waters.
The language of fish
cut out at the root.
Mute oceans. Oil like a gag
on the Gulf of Mexico . . .

A woodpecker heckled.
A vulture picked at its own breast.
Thrice from the cockerel, as per.
The macaw squawked:
Nouns I know –
Rain. Forest. Fire. Ash.
Chainsaw. Cattle. Cocaine. Cash.
Squatters. Ranchers. Loggers. Looters.
Barons. Shooters.

A hawk swore.
A nightingale opened its throat
in a garbled quote.
A worm turned in the blackbird's beak.
This from the crane:
What I saw – slow thaw
in permafrost; broken terrain
of mud and lakes;
peat broth; seepage; melt;
methane breath.

A bat hung like a suicide.
Only a rasp of wings from the raven.
A heron was stone; a robin blood
in the written wood.
So snow and darkness slowly fell;
the eagle, history, in silhouette,
with the golden plover,
and the albatross
                    telling of Arctic ice
as the cold, hard moon calved from the earth.

CAROL ANN DUFFY

For the House Sparrow, In Decline

Your numbers fall and it's tempting to think
you're deserting our suburbs and estates
like your cousins at Pompeii; that when you return
to bathe in dust and build your nests again
in a roofless world where no one hears your *cheeps*,
only a starling's modem mimicry
will remind you of how you once supplied
the incidental music of our lives.

PAUL FARLEY

Explaining an Affinity for Bats

That they are only glimpsed in silhouette,
And seem something else at first – a swallow –
And move like new tunes, difficult to follow,
Staggering towards an obstacle they yet
Avoid in a last-minute pirouette,
Somehow telling solid things from hollow,
Sounding out how high a space, or shallow,
Revising into deepening violet.

That they sing – not the way the songbird sings
(Whose song is rote, to ornament, finesse) –
But travel by a sort of song that rings
True not in utterance, but harkenings,
Who find their way by calling into darkness
To hear their voice bounce off the shape of things.

A. E. STALLINGS

The Late Wasp

You that through all the dying summer
Came every morning to our breakfast table,
A lonely bachelor mummer,
And fed on the marmalade
So deeply, all your strength was scarcely able
To prise you from the sweet pit you had made, –
You and the earth have now grown older,
And your blue thoroughfares have felt a change;
They have grown colder;
And it is strange
How the familiar avenues of the air
Crumble now, crumble; the good air will not hold,
All cracked and perished with the cold;
And down you dive through nothing and through despair.

EDWIN MUIR

The Red Admiral

The wings tremble, it is the red admiral
Ecstatically against the garden wall;
September is his enjoyment, but he does not know it,
Name it, or refer to it at all.

The old light fades upon the old stones;
The day is old: how is there such light
From grey clouds? It is the autumnal equinox,
And we shall all have shrunk before daylight.

A woman, a horse and a walnut tree: old voices
Out of recessed time, in the cracks,
It may be, where the plaster has crumbled:
But the butterfly hugs the blue lias.

The mystery is only the close of day,
Remembered love, which is also present:
Layer upon layer, old times, the fish turning
Once more in the pond, and the absent.

All could not be at once without memory
Crowding out what cannot be remembered;
Better to have none, best of all when
The evening sunlight has ended.

Its finger lighter than spiders, the red admiral
Considers, as I do, with little movement;
With little of anything that is meant:
But let the meaning go, movement is all.

C. H.SISSON

Leafcutter Bees

Perhaps the wrens were having a go at some kind of abstract beauty.
Anyhow they built a nest they didn't use in the thick yew-tree.
And a few days afterwards when someone gave it a poke
With a concerted high-pitched buzz the dim thing spoke.
Little gold bees like quarter-scale bumbles
Tumbled out of it in response to the fumbles.
"Oh the little darlings" some female utters,
"Leave them alone, they're only leaf-cutters,
They won't harm your potherbs or your posies,
Only cut round holes in the leaves of the roses."
Huh! They by-passed the roses as if they'd been nettles.
They wrapped up their eggs in geranium petals.
They took a dead set at a thing that really matters,
They cut the flame geraniums into shreds and tatters.
We knew where they lived. We could have gone at night
And done them all in and served them all right.
But we could not penalise them for their childish folly,
Any more than little girls who want to dress their dolly,
Who take their little scissors and with uncertain
Snips cut a great piece from your red silk curtain.

RUTH PITTER

3rd July: Gift

A noise is on the loose today;
black winding pendulum weight of core
by the main road to Radstock.
I take a saw to cut down the bough of a swarm.

The air's innards have sprung apart.
I am netted in trawls of strumming bee.
Can I say
what kind of halo absorbs me?

In and in and in a morass, fast place, race,
roadside and twenty years of brittle bramble
thick with bees,
thorns snagging my beekeeper's costume.

I did not expect a calm lack of resistance like this.
Not one sting as I handle fizzing thousands,

entering the physiology of a heatwave;
their aspect, divine as electrons;
physically deranged sound
like a fool holding its freedom.

You *are* winged strange kind, you are nerval.
Inside your fluency,
mirrors facing all mirrors shade back to eternity.

Standing in the middle of your intellect:
must catch and keep.
My shroud conceals a skeleton of tensions, not me; I'm right out
in the open livid whirlpool of metropolis rid of its rooms.

I bring this hive,
Come in.

Bees from hands drop slowly as honey.
I close the lid on them, I wish the willing in.

Bring in a sound like Hestia, like hearth, like heart.

And they convey
the queen flame through the door.
I'd swear
you are descendants of the dead that swarmed last year
from here;
the width of your banding, that particular
taper of abdomen, colour . . .

I leave the box to gain its anima.

Now, darkfall, I return to claim.
Detect
new-trying gritty clicky voice of thousands;
a chord of assembly tuning its domestic.
(Note, each colony different,
an amicable pitch inside all else.)

I listen
to the insular, poached wild body under the bonnet.

Finder, keeper. Life's instrument.

This in my arms (this heavy box) I take to the apiary.
I look at the road we have to cross.
You are not fully ordinary, bees.
The ordinary mortals go by in cars.

SEAN BORODALE

The Stare's Nest by My Window

The bees build in the crevices
Of loosening masonry, and there
The mother birds bring grubs and flies.
My wall is loosening; honey-bees
Come build in the empty house of the stare.

We are closed in, and the key is turned
On our uncertainty; somewhere
A man is killed, or a house burned,
Yet no clear fact to be discerned:
Come build in the empty house of the stare.

A barricade of stone or of wood;
Some fourteen days of civil war;
Last night they trundled down the road
That dead young soldier in his blood:
Come build in the empty house of the stare.

We had fed the heart on fantasies,
The heart's grown brutal from the fare;
More substance in our enmities
Than in our love; O honey-bees
Come build in the empty house of the stare.

W. B. YEATS

The Host

While I have been away the fruit flies
have moved in with their extended family
and rise politely off a feast of black
banana skin to welcome me home. I swat
and slap, but they just laugh on the updraft
of my flapping, batting hands.

The banana gone, I open a window, hoping
they will make off to some other repast
but they post a halo round my head,
two hundred wingbeats to a second, hatched
with a brain far quicker than mine. At my desk,
I am possessed, follow the threads for evidence

of pestilence, the death of civilisations
by Zebub, Arob, all the dust of Egypt
turned to gnats that torment livestock, squat
on ruined crop, rotted fish and frog.
In the face of this invasion, I am
an avenger sent to stop a plague,

enter *Kill Fruit Flies*, study the traps, fill
a glass jar with cider vinegar, stir in sugar,
cover with cunning cling-film, pierce and wait,
and they come, hover like decorous guests
at a table, perch on the rim. I watch them drown
one by one, then return to my desk. But just

as I begin to write, one rises up at the edge
of my sight like the crop-duster in North
by Northwest. I spin back into battle, set
the trap again, more delicious, more sugar, more
stealth. It sits on the lip, licks at the cling-film,
sips. I strike. It dies a vinegar death.

Through the rest of the day I revisit the site.
No sign of return. The next morning no one
is there, the jar untouched, my table bare
in the desolate kitchen. I try to work but keep
coming back to stand like an expectant host,
waiting to welcome the guest I miss.

IMTIAZ DHARKER

the beginning of the end of the world

cockroach population possibly declining
– News Report

maybe the morning the roaches
walked into the kitchen
bold with they bad selves
marching up out of the drains
not like soldiers   like priests
grim and patient in the sink
and when we ran the water
trying to drown them as if they were
soldiers   they seemed to bow their
sad heads   for us not at us
and march single file away

maybe then   the morning we rose
from our beds as always
listening for the bang of the end
of the world   maybe then
when we heard only the tiny tapping
and saw them dark and prayerful
in the kitchen   maybe then
when we watched them turn from us
faithless at last
and walk in a long line away

LUCILLE CLIFTON

Cold Blooded Creatures

Man, the egregious egoist
(In mystery the twig is bent),
Imagines, by some mental twist,
That he alone is sentient

Of the intolerable load
Which on all living creatures lies,
Nor stoops to pity in the toad
The speechless sorrow of its eyes.

He asks no questions of the snake,
Nor plumbs the phosphorescent gloom
Where lidless fishes, broad awake,
Swim staring at a nightmare doom.

ELINOR WYLIE

from The Fish, the Man, and the Spirit

TO FISH

You strange, astonished-looking, angle-faced,
Dreary-mouthed, gaping wretches of the sea,
Gulping salt-water everlastingly,
Cold-blooded, though with red your blood be graced,
And mute, though dwellers in the roaring waste;
And you, all shapes beside, that fishy be, –
Some round, some flat, some long, all devilry,
Legless, unloving, infamously chaste: –

O scaly, slippery, wet, swift, staring wights,
What is't ye do? What life lead? eh, dull goggles?
How do ye vary your vile days and nights?
How pass your Sundays? Are ye still but joggles
In ceaseless wash? Still naught but gapes and bites,
And drinks, and stares, diversified with boggles?

A FISH ANSWERS

Amazing monster! that, for aught I know,
With the first sight of thee didst make our race
For ever stare! O flat and shocking face,
Grimly divided from the breast below!
Thou that on dry land horribly dost go
With a split body and most ridiculous pace,
Prong after prong, disgracer of all grace,
Long-useless-finn'd, haired, upright, unwet, slow!

O breather of unbreathable, sword-sharp air,
How canst exist? How bear thyself, thou dry
And dreary sloth? What particles can share
Of the only blessed life, the watery?
I sometimes see of ye an actual *pair*
Go by! linked fin by fin! most odiously.

LEIGH HUNT

Basking Shark

To stub an oar on a rock where none should be,
To have it rise with a slounge out of the sea
Is a thing that happened once (too often) to me.

But not too often – though enough. I count as gain
That once I met, on a sea tin-tacked with rain,
That roomsized monster with a matchbox brain.

He displaced more than water. He shoggled me
Centuries back – this decadent townee
Shook on a wrong branch of his family tree.

Swish up the dirt and, when it settles, a spring
Is all the clearer. I saw me, in one fling,
Emerging from the slime of everything.

So who's the monster? The thought made me grow pale
For twenty seconds while, sail after sail,
The tall fin slid away and then the tail.

NORMAN MACCAIG

Anecdote of the Squid

The squid is in fact
a carnivorous pocket
containing a pen, which serves
the squid as his skeleton.

The squid is a raised finger or
an opposed thumb. The squid's quill
is his long, scrupulous nail, which
is invisible.

The squid is a short-beaked
bird who has eaten
his single wing, or impaled
himself on his feather.

The squid, however,
despite his Cadurcian
wineskin and 400 cups,
does not entertain.

The squid, with his eight
arms and his two
brushes and his sepia,
does not draw.

The squid knows too that the use
of pen and ink is neither recording
impressions nor signing his name
to forms and petitions.

But the squid may be said,
for instance, to transcribe
his silence into the space
between seafloor and wave,

or to invoke an unspoken
word, whose muscular
nonpronunciation the squid
alone is known to have mastered.

The squid carries his ink
in a sack, not a bottle.
With it the squid makes
artifacts.

These are mistakable for
portraiture, or
for self-portraiture, or,
to the eyes of the squid-eating whale,

for the squid, who, in the meanwhile grows
transparent and withdraws,
leaving behind him his
coagulating shadows.

ROBERT BRINGHURST

The Starfish

creeps like expired meat –
fizzy-skinned, pentamerously-legged,
her underfur of sucking feet
shivers upon an immobile mussel
whose navy mackintosh is zipped
against the anchor of this fat paw,
this seemingly soft nutcracker who exerts
such pressure until the mussel's jaw
drops a single millimetre. Into this cleft
she'll press the shopping bag of her stomach
and turn the mollusc into broth,
haul in the goods and stumble off,
leaving a vacant cubicle,
a prayer come apart.

ISABEL GALLEYMORE

The Snake

A snake came to my water-trough,
On a hot, hot day, and I in pyjamas for the heat,
To drink there.

In the deep, strange-scented shade of the great dark carob-tree
I came down the steps with my pitcher
And must wait, must stand and wait, for there he was at the trough
before me.

He reached down from a fissure in the earth-wall in the gloom
And trailed his yellow-brown slackness soft-bellied down over the
edge of the stone trough.
And rested his throat upon the stone bottom,
And where the water had dripped from the tap, in a small clearness,
He sipped with his straight mouth,
Softly drank through his straight gums, into his slack long body,
Silently.

Someone was before me at my water-trough,
And I, like a second comer, waiting.

He lifted his head from his drinking, like cattle do,
And looked at me vaguely, as drinking cattle do,
And flickered his two-forked tongue from his lips, and mused
a moment,
And stooped and drank a little more,
Being earth-brown, earth-golden from the burning bowels of
the earth
On the day of Sicilian July, with Etna smoking.

The voice of my education said to me
He must be killed.
For in Sicily the black, black snakes are innocent, the gold are
venomous.

And voices in me said, if you were a man
You would take a stick and break him now, and finish him off.

But I must confess how I liked him,
How glad I was he had come like a guest in quiet, to drink at my
water-trough
And depart peaceful, pacified and thankless,
Into the burning bowels of this earth.

Was it cowardice, that I dared not kill him?
Was it perversity, that I longed to talk to him?
Was it humility, to feel so honoured?
I felt so honoured.

And yet those voices:
If you were not afraid, you would kill him!

And truly I was afraid, I was most afraid,
But even so, honoured still more
That he should seek my hospitality
From out the dark door of the secret earth.

He drank enough
And lifted his head, dreamily, as one who has drunken,
And flickered his tongue like a forked night on the air, so black,
Seeming to lick his lips,
And looking around like a god, unseeing, into the air,
And slowly turned his head,
And slowly, very slowly, as if thrice adream,
Proceeded to draw his slow length curving round
And climb again the broken bank of my wall-face.

And as he put his head into that dreadful hole,
And as he slowly drew up, snake-easing his shoulders, and entered
farther,
A sort of horror, a sort of protest against his withdrawing into that
horrid black hole,

Deliberately going into the blackness, and slowly drawing himself
after,
Overcame me now his back was turned.

I looked around, I put down my pitcher,
I picked up a clumsy log
And threw it at the water-trough with a clatter.

I think I did not hit him,
But suddenly that part of him that was left behind convulsed in
undignified haste,
Writhed like lightning, and was gone
Into the black hole, the earth-lipped fissure in the wall-front,
At which, in the intense still noon, I stared with fascination.

And immediately I regretted it.
I thought how paltry, how vulgar, what a mean act!
I despised myself and the voices of my accursed human education.

And I thought of the albatross,
And I wished he would come back, my snake.

For he seemed to me again like a king,
Like a king in exile, uncrowned in the underworld,
Now due to be crowned again.

And so, I missed my chance with one of the lords
Of life.
And I have something to expiate;
A pettiness.

D. H. LAWRENCE

A Narrow Fellow in the Grass

A narrow Fellow in the Grass
Occasionally rides –
You may have met Him – did you not
His notice instant is –

The Grass divides as with a Comb –
A spotted Shaft is seen –
And then it closes at your Feet
And opens further on –

He likes a Boggy Acre
A Floor too cool for Corn –
But when a Boy and Barefoot –
I more than once at Noon

Have passed, I thought, a Whip Lash
Unbraiding in the Sun
When stooping to secure it
It wrinkled, and was gone –

Several of Nature's People
I know, and they know me –
I feel for them a transport
Of cordiality –

But never met this Fellow
Attended, or alone
Without a tighter breathing
And Zero at the Bone –

EMILY DICKINSON

Toad

Stop looking like a purse. How could a purse
squeeze under the rickety door and sit,
full of satisfaction, in a man's house?

You clamber towards me on your four corners –
right hand, left foot, left hand, right foot.

I love you for being a toad,
for crawling like a Japanese wrestler,
and for not being frightened.

I put you in my purse hand, not shutting it,
and set you down outside directly under
every star.

A jewel in your head? Toad,
you've put one in mine,
a tiny radiance in a dark place.

NORMAN MACCAIG

The Moose

for Grace Bulmer Bowers

From narrow provinces
of fish and bread and tea,
home of the long tides
where the bay leaves the sea
twice a day and takes
the herrings long rides,

where if the river
enters or retreats
in a wall of brown foam
depends on if it meets
the bay coming in,
the bay not at home;

where, silted red,
sometimes the sun sets
facing a red sea,
and others, veins the flats'
lavender, rich mud
in burning rivulets;

on red, gravelly roads,
down rows of sugar maples,
past clapboard farmhouses
and neat, clapboard churches,
bleached, ridged as clamshells,
past twin silver birches,

through late afternoon
a bus journeys west,
the windshield flashing pink,
pink glancing off of metal,
brushing the dented flank
of blue, beat-up enamel;

down hollows, up rises,
and waits, patient, while
a lone traveller gives
kisses and embraces
to seven relatives
and a collie supervises.

Goodbye to the elms,
to the farm, to the dog.
The bus starts. The light
grows richer; the fog,
shifting, salty, thin,
comes closing in.

Its cold, round crystals
form and slide and settle
in the white hens' feathers,
in gray glazed cabbages,
on the cabbage roses
and lupins like apostles;

the sweet peas cling
to their wet white string
on the whitewashed fences;
bumblebees creep
inside the foxgloves,
and evening commences.

One stop at Bass River.
Then the Economies
Lower, Middle, Upper;
Five Islands, Five Houses,
where a woman shakes a tablecloth
out after supper.

A pale flickering. Gone.
The Tantramar marshes
and the smell of salt hay.
An iron bridge trembles
and a loose plank rattles
but doesn't give way.

On the left, a red light
swims through the dark:
a ship's port lantern.
Two rubber boots show,
illuminated, solemn.
A dog gives one bark.

A woman climbs in
with two market bags,
brisk, freckled, elderly.
'A grand night. Yes, sir,
all the way to Boston.'
She regards us amicably.

Moonlight as we enter
the New Brunswick woods,
hairy, scratchy, splintery;
moonlight and mist
caught in them like lamb's wool
on bushes in a pasture.

The passengers lie back.
Snores. Some long sighs.
A dreamy divagation
begins in the night,
a gentle, auditory,
slow hallucination . . .

In the creakings and noises,
an old conversation
– not concerning us,
but recognizable, somewhere,
back in the bus:
Grandparents' voices

uninterruptedly
talking, in Eternity:
names being mentioned,
things cleared up finally;
what he said, what she said,
who got pensioned;

deaths, deaths and sicknesses;
the year he remarried;
the year (something) happened.
She died in childbirth.
That was the son lost
when the schooner foundered.

He took to drink. Yes.
She went to the bad.
When Amos began to pray
even in the store and
finally the family had
to put him away.

'Yes . . .' that peculiar
affirmative. 'Yes . . .'
A sharp, indrawn breath,
half groan, half acceptance,
that means 'Life's like that.
We know *it* (also death).'

Talking the way they talked
in the old featherbed,
peacefully, on and on,
dim lamplight in the hall,
down in the kitchen, the dog
tucked in her shawl.

Now, it's all right now
even to fall asleep
just as on all those nights.
– Suddenly the bus driver
stops with a jolt,
turns off his lights.

A moose has come out of
the impenetrable wood
and stands there, looms, rather,
in the middle of the road.
It approaches; it sniffs at
the bus's hot hood.

Towering, antlerless,
high as a church,
homely as a house
(or, safe as houses).
A man's voice assures us
'Perfectly harmless . . .'

Some of the passengers
exclaim in whispers,
childishly, softly,
'Sure are big creatures.'
'It's awful plain.'
'Look! It's a she!'

Taking her time,
she looks the bus over,
grand, otherworldly.
Why, why do we feel
(we all feel) this sweet
sensation of joy?

'Curious creatures,'
says our quiet driver,
rolling his *r*'s.
'Look at that, would you.'
Then he shifts gears.
For a moment longer,

by craning backward,
the moose can be seen
on the moonlit macadam;
then there's a dim
smell of moose, an acrid
smell of gasoline.

ELIZABETH BISHOP

Fox

You don't ever know where
a sentence will take you, depending
on its roll and fold. I was walking
over the dunes when I saw
the red fox asleep under the green
branches of the pine. It flared up
in the sweet order of its being,
the tail that was over the muzzle
lifting in airy amazement
and the fire of the eyes followed
and the pricked ears and the thin
barrel body and the four
athletic legs in their black stockings and it
came to me how the polish of the world changes
everything. I was hot I was cold I was almost
dead of delight. Of course the mind keeps
cool in its hidden palace – yes, the mind takes
a long time, is otherwise occupied than by
happiness, and deep breathing. Still,
at last, it comes too, running
like a wild thing, to be taken
with its twin sister, breath. So I stood
on the pale, peach-colored sand, watching the fox
as it opened like a flower, and I began
softly, to pick among the vast assortment of words
that it should run again and again across the page
that you again and again should shiver with praise.

MARY OLIVER

The Buck in the Snow

White sky, over the hemlocks bowed with snow,
Saw you not at the beginning of evening the antlered buck and
his doe
Standing in the apple-orchard? I saw them. I saw them suddenly go,
Tails up, with long leaps lovely and slow,
Over the stone-wall into the wood of hemlocks bowed with snow.

Now lies he here, his wild blood scalding the snow.

How strange a thing is death, bringing to his knees, bringing to
his antlers
The buck in the snow.
How strange a thing, – a mile away by now, it may be,
Under the heavy hemlocks that as the moments pass
Shift their loads a little, letting fall a feather of snow –
Life, looking out attentive from the eyes of the doe.

EDNA ST VINCENT MILLAY

The Deer

It came from trying to make sense of a shadow.
A faltering mirage in the engine's steam
which stood vibrating on the tarmac,
illuminated by the headlights
as we peeled to a halt –
neither brave nor afraid
but unmoving in an unnerving way.

His pointed eyes, like currants,
protruding from a velveteen forehead
bore through the windshield
despite the darkness.
We hadn't seen signs of life in hours
apart from live oaks elaborating
soundless in the distance.

Straining brought him into focus,
fur bristling in the minor wind.
Exposed pedicles from antlers shed,
seasonal holes in the skull ringing
where true bone had born away.
His legs tense, unaccustomed to rest
and angled in a bad way.

I had never heard a deer scream,
like a whining gone sharp and sour.
Had no clue how to comfort or silence
the sound that trailed after me.
Until morning broke with a start
and a yolky sun pierced the horizon,
illuminating hoof prints scorched in the dirt.

JESS MCKINNEY

Pigs

Us all on sore cement was we.
Not warmed then with glares. Not glutting mush
under that pole the lightning's tied to.
No farrow-shit in milk to make us randy.
Us back in cool god-shit. We ate crisp.
We nosed up good rank in the tunnelled bush.
Us all fuckers then. And Big, huh? Tusked
the balls-biting dog and gutsed him wet.
Us shoved down the soft cement of rivers.
Us snored the earth hollow, filled farrow, grunted.
Never stopped growing. We sloughed, we soughed
and balked no weird till the high ridgebacks was us
with weight-buried hooves. Or bristly, with milk.
Us never knowed like slitting nor hose-biff then.
Not the terrible body-cutting screams up ahead.
The burnt water kicking. This gone-already feeling
here in no place with our heads on upside down.

LES MURRAY

The Hunter

He set out and kept hunting
and hunting. Where, he thought
and thought, is the real chamois?
and can I kill it where it is?
He had brought with him only a dish
of pears. The autumn wind soared
above the trails where the drops
of the chamois led him further.
The leaves dropped around him
like pie-plates. The stars fell
one by one into his eyes and burnt.

There is a geography which holds
its hands just so far from the breast
and pushes you away, crying so.
He went on to strange hills where
the stones were still warm from feet,
and then on and on. There were clouds
at his knees, his eyelashes
had grown thick with the colds,
as the fur of the bear does
in winter. Perhaps, he thought, I am
asleep, but he did not freeze to death.

There were little green needles
everywhere. And then manna fell.
He knew, above all, that he was now
approved, and his strength increased.
He saw the world below him, brilliant
as a floor, and steaming with gold,
with distance. There were occasionally
rifts in the cloud where the face
of a woman appeared, frowning. He
had gone higher. He wore ermine.
He thought, why did I come? and then,
I have come to rule! The chamois came.

The chamois came and they came
in droves to humiliate him. Alone,
in the clouds, he was humiliated.

FRANK O'HARA

The Donkey

It was such a pretty little donkey
It had such pretty ears
And it used to gallop rounds the field so briskly
Though well down in years.

It was a retired donkey,
After a life-time of working
Between the shafts of regular employment
It was now free to go merrymaking.

Oh in its eyes was such a gleam
As is usually associated with youth
But it was not a youthful gleam really,
But full of mature truth.

And of the hilarity that goes with age,
As if to tell us sardonically
No hedged track lay before this donkey longer
But the sweet prairies of anarchy.

But the sweet prairies of anarchy
And the thought that keeps my heart up
That at last, in Death's odder anarchy,
Our pattern will be broken all up.
Though precious we are momentarily, donkey,
I aspire to be broken up.

STEVIE SMITH

Hedgehog

The snail moves like a
Hovercraft, held up by a
Rubber cushion of itself,
Sharing its secret

With the hedgehog. The hedgehog
Shares its secret with no one.
We say, Hedgehog, come out
Of yourself and we will love you.

We mean no harm. We want
Only to listen to what
You have to say. We want
Your answers to our questions.

The hedgehog gives nothing
Away, keeping itself to itself.
We wonder what a hedgehog
Has to hide, why it so distrusts.

We forget the god
Under this crown of thorns.
We forget that never again
Will a god trust in the world.

PAUL MULDOON

Mole

Those new flagstones need undermining,
the concrete sundial could use a tilt and while he's at it
he'll make a disaster of the borders. His order
is not our order. He prays to his own ingenuity. His desires
feature a plump worm larder and to gather
the tender beechnuts while avoiding horrors the surface
churns out: cat-things, dog-things, pellet guns, poison,
trowels to flip him over the fence into the neighbour's
as though that doesn't hurt. It doesn't *work* for us,
his gross body plan, eyes skinned over and his front feet
hands, polydactylic and psychoanalytically proportioned
in that they are oversized and hairless. He does not require
an afterlife. When the consequence whose birth
we've outsourced, raised *extra muros* on the output
of our comfort zone comes of age, he will simply return
to his live/work situation as the manager and sole proprietor
of our old estates. He'll raise each molehill like a flag.
In the morning the lawn will be a field of victory.

KAREN SOLIE

Black Bear in the Grocery Store

here we are in Thousand Oaks –
cypress trees in the grue distance –
milk in one hand and the other out-
stretched
fetching
when we are stupefied in the land of plenty
of aisles and aisles of having
what is canned   bottled   preserved   fresh
all must be paid for
in this tiled valley of dead things
between steel streams full with multi-coloured plastic
and paper packages and tin flowers
and below the m&ms and loo roll and ramen
a black bear – barely a yearling – so hot
she cannot calibrate sleep
maw open
she places paw
before paw
her bow-legged limbs all limber and lank
her cinnamon snout bearing low
in search of –
I make a list –
bird food and garbage
water and same-day salmon
here
in this counterfeit den
with its cool cool weather
she moves
that we might see her and do more
than spill our cold milk

TJAWANGWA DEMA

from Walking to the Cattle Place

A Meditation

5. *Death Words*

Beasts, cattle, have words, neither minor nor many.
The most frightening comes with a sudden stilt jump: the blood-moan
straight out of earth's marrow, that *clameur*, huge-mouthed,
raised when they nose death at one of their own

and only then. The whole milking herd at that cry
will come galloping, curveting, fish-leaping in furious play-steps
on the thunderstruck paddock, horning one another. A hock dance.
A puddle of blood will trigger it, even afterbirth.

They make the shield-wall over it, the foreheads jam down
on where death has stuck, as if to horn to death Death
(dumb rising numerous straw-trace). They pour out strength
enormously on the place, heap lungs' heat on the dead one.

It is one word they enact in the horn-gate there
and the neighbour herds all running to join in it
hit the near fences, creaking. We've unpicked many million
variants from our own like wake. This is a sample.

Roughly all at once, though, from the last-comers inward
the bunched rite breaks up. They grow aimless, calm down
in straggling completion. You might say Eat, missa est.
It is uttered just once for each charnel. They will feed

a tongue's nub away from then on. Their word of power
is formal, terrible, but, for an age now, stops there.
At best, ours ramify still. Perhaps God is inevitable.
He will not necessarily come, though, again, in our species.

LES MURRAY

The Mad Cow Believes She Is the Spirit of the Weather

People out walking lean into the wind, the rain:
they believe it thwarts the weather to welcome it like that.
I can happily get lost for hours in a swirl of showers
because I was born into weather. They still tell
how my mother pushed me out of her body
on to a rock and I split the stone in two while the rain
washed me and the thunder broke overhead.
I was a junior cloud goddess, with storms following
me, winds and whirlwinds, shots of rain
and a split sky above my head. Always moving,
I kept one jump ahead of getting wet, kicking
back at the clouds with my hind legs
to keep them there. It's harder now, here
in the future: my brain has the characteristics
of a sponge and the rain seeps into the holes.
I think I'm making chaos. My vests
don't keep me warm and when I last sneezed
a volcano in the Pacific threw a sheet of dust
around the world. I'm dangerous to the earth.
I spat and a blanket of algae four miles long
bloomed on the Cornish coast. I rubbed
the sleep from my eyes and a meteor large enough
to make the earth wobble in its orbit
came very close indeed. I have been sad recently
and now the weather has changed for good.

JO SHAPCOTT

Neighbours

That spring was late. We watched the sky
and studied charts for shouldering isobars.
Birds were late to pair. Crows drank from the lamb's eye.

Over Finland small birds fell: song-thrushes
steering north, smudged signatures on light,
migrating warblers, nightingales.

Wing-beats failed over fjords, each lung a sip of gall.
Children were warned of their dangerous beauty.
Milk was spilt in Poland. Each quarrel

the blowback from some old story,
a mouthful of bitter air from the Ukraine
brought by the wind out of its box of sorrows.

This spring a lamb sips caesium on a Welsh hill.
A child, lifting her face to drink the rain,
takes into her blood the poisoned arrow.

Now we are all neighbourly, each little town
in Europe twinned to Chernobyl, each heart
with the burnt fireman, the child on the Moscow train.

In the democracy of the virus and the toxin
we wait. We watch for bird migrations,
one bird returning with green in its voice,

glasnost,
golau glas,*
a first break of blue.

* golau glas: blue light

GILLIAN CLARKE

In California: Morning, Evening, Late January

Pale, then enkindled,
light
advancing,
emblazoning
summits of palm and pine,

the dew
lingering,
scripture of
scintillas.

Soon the roar
of mowers
cropping the already short
grass of lawns,

men with long-nozzled
cylinders of pesticide
poking at weeds,
at moss in cracks of cement,

and louder roar
of helicopters off to spray
vineyards where *braceros* try
to hold their breath,

and in the distance, bulldozers, excavators,
babel of destructive construction.

Banded by deep
oakshadow, airy
shadow of eucalyptus,

miner's lettuce,
tender, untasted,
and other grass, unmown,
luxuriant,
no green more brilliant.

Fragile paradise.

. . . .

At day's end the whole sky,
vast, unstinting, flooded with transparent
mauve,
tint of wisteria,
cloudless
over the malls, the industrial parks,
the homes with the lights going on,
the homeless arranging their bundles.

. . . .

Who can utter
the poignance of all that is constantly
threatened, invaded, expended

and constantly
nevertheless
persists in beauty,

tranquil as this young moon
just risen and slowly
drinking light
from the vanished sun.

Who can utter
the praise of such generosity
or the shame?

DENISE LEVERTOV

Unbeliever

Nowhere in these wildflower shuddering meadows,
mindless, mindless in the wind's demands,

or the long, thin waterfalls pluming off the cliffs
like ponies' tails,

or the cornices of snow, impossibly, snow,
enduring in depressions, or down the fanned folds

those summits comprise,
can I see what I'm told has happened already

happening in sight. Not even in spirit
do I feel an ending

under the twinned swags of the cable cars
and the weeping pines

that mat the steep slopes
and encroach upon the village,

so close – like this – to Rilke's grave
and rocks that Ruskin must have loved, if he came

this way, have loved, and drawn.
Persistent world! – the river sprints past it,

the valley crowds round, and I know what I know
as well as I can say it,

but never can grasp
that bathers pummelled by pearly jets

in geothermal pools,
tilting their chins to the sun,

will not keep bobbing for a thousand years to come,
their naked shoulders

colouring and colouring, like roses,
but never quite burned.

FRANCES LEVISTON

There's a Certain Slant of Light

There's a certain Slant of light,
Winter Afternoons –
That oppresses like the Heft
Of Cathedral Tunes –

Heavenly Hurt, it gives us –
We can find no scar,
But internal difference,
Where the Meanings, are –

None may teach it – Any –
'Tis the Seal Despair –
An imperial affliction
Sent us of the Air –

When it comes, the Landscape listens –
Shadows – hold their breath –
When it goes 'tis like the Distance
On the look of Death –

EMILY DICKINSON

Snow

The room was suddenly rich and the great bay-window was
Spawning snow and pink roses against it
Soundlessly collateral and incompatible:
World is suddener than we fancy it.

World is crazier and more of it than we think,
Incorrigibly plural. I peel and portion
A tangerine and spit the pips and feel
the drunkenness of things being various.

And the fire flames with a bubbling sound for world
Is more spiteful and gay than one supposes –
On the tongue on the eyes on the ears in the palms of one's hands –
There is more than glass between the snow and the huge roses.

LOUIS MACNEICE

Inversnaid

This darksome burn, horseback brown,
His rollrock highroad roaring down,
In coop and in comb the fleece of his foam
Flutes and low to the lake falls home.

A windpuff-bonnet of fáwn-fróth
Turns and twindles over the broth
Of a pool so pitchblack, féll-frówning,
It rounds and rounds Despair to drowning.

Degged with dew, dappled with dew
Are the groins of the braes that the brook treads through,
Wiry heathpacks, flitches of fern,
And the beadbonny ash that sits over the burn.

What would the world be, once bereft
Of wet and of wildness? Let them be left,
O let them be left, wildness and wet;
Long live the weeds and the wilderness yet.

GERARD MANLEY HOPKINS

from The Mores

These paths are stopped – the rude philistine's thrall
Is laid upon them and destroyed them all.
Each little tyrant with his little sign
Shows where man claims, earth glows no more divine.
On paths to freedom and to childhood dear
A board sticks up to notice 'no road here'
And on the tree with ivy overhung
The hated sign by vulgar taste is hung
As though the very birds should learn to know
When they go there they must no further go.
Thus, with the poor, scared freedom bade good-bye
And much they feel it in the smothered sigh,
And birds and trees and flowers without a name
All sighed when lawless law's enclosure came,
And dreams of plunder in such rebel schemes
Have found too truly that they were but dreams.

JOHN CLARE

Death of a Field

The field itself is lost the morning it becomes a site
When the Notice goes up: Fingal County Council – 44 houses

The memory of the field is lost with the loss of its herbs

Though the woodpigeons in the willow
The finches in what's left of the hawthorn hedge
And the wagtail in the elder
Sing on their hungry summer song

The magpies sound like flying castanets

And the memory of the field disappears with its flora:
Who can know the yearning of yarrow
Or the plight of the scarlet pimpernel
Whose true colour is orange?

The end of the field is the end of the hidey holes
Where first smokes, first tokes, first gropes
Were had to the scentless mayweed

The end of the field as we know it is the start of the estate
The site to be planted with houses each two- or three-bedroom
Nest of sorrow and chemical, cargo of joy

The end of dandelion is the start of Flash
The end of dock is the start of Pledge
The end of teazel is the start of Ariel
The end of primrose is the start of Brillo
The end of thistle is the start of Bounce
The end of sloe is the start of Oxyaction
The end of herb robert is the start of Brasso
The end of eyebright is the start of Persil

Who amongst us is able to number the end of grasses
To number the losses of each seeding head?

I'll walk out once
Barefoot under the moon to know the field
Through the soles of my feet to hear
The myriad leaf lives green and singing
The million million cycles of being in wing

That – before the field become map memory
In some archive on some architect's screen
I might possess it or it possess me
Through its night dew, its moon-white caul
Its slick and shine and its profligacy
In every wingbeat in every beat of time

PAULA MEEHAN

Innocence

They laughed at one I loved –
The triangular hill that hung
Under the Big Forth. They said
That I was bounded by the whitethorn hedges
Of the little farm and did not know the world.
But I knew that love's doorway to life
Is the same doorway everywhere.

Ashamed of what I loved
I flung her from me and called her a ditch
Although she was smiling at me with violets.

But now I am back in her briary arms;
The dew of an Indian Summer morning lies
On bleached potato-stalks –
What age am I?

I do not know what age I am,
I am no mortal age;
I know nothing of women,
Nothing of cities,
I cannot die
Unless I walk outside these whitethorn hedges.

PATRICK KAVANAGH

earth cries

she doesn't cry for water
she runs rivers deep
she doesn't cry for food
she has suckled trees
she doesn't cry for clothing
she weaves all that she wears
she doesn't cry for shelter
she grows thatch everywhere
she doesn't cry for children
she's got more than she can bear
she doesn't cry for heaven
she knows it's always there
you don't know why she's crying
when she's got everything
how could you know she's crying
for just one humane being

JEAN 'BINTA' BREEZE

Iceberg Season

The icebergs arrive in their beautiful veils.
They drift along the aisles
of the sound with creaks and growls

seeking a warmth that will finish them.
We crowd onto cliff-tops to see them
and wonder at their overhangs

which birds love; kittiwakes and gulls
run amok, tricked into thinking
they've found a new home.

They are in our sights for weeks –
a gentle company that's bolder
when the moon is old and curdled

and keeps us all from sleep. As long as
they are with us we believe, and we weep
as we pray to the god of cold.

KATHARINE TOWERS

The Summit

When I met the glacier face to face
there was no coming together
of skin and ice,
just washy clouds and a weepy sky
floating upside down
in a silver lake, and the eyes
looking up from the water were mine.

It was a hard slog
in a valley more like a Scottish Glen,
along hillsides more at home
in the English Lakes.
A day's trek up a narrow track
between harebell and birch
and to do what:

to say that the Arctic looks like this
or looks like that, to breathe
its cool breath then scratch a name
in the visitors' book
and give the place a human form:
tongue, body, mouth and heart . . .
in any event

I was too late.
Looking up from the milky pool
I saw the whiteness in retreat,
the bedraggled hem of the bridal train
heading into the heights
towards deeper winter and truer north,
trailing a stony path.

When I met the glacier face to face
there was no close encounter
of ancient snow and body heat,
just weepy clouds and a washy sky
hanging upside down
in a zinc-coloured lake, and the eyes
staring out of the water were mine.

SIMON ARMITAGE

Everest

Once it was Chomolungma,
Mother Goddess of the Earth,
a face whose veil rarely lifted,
its whiteness the White Whale's.

Now it's like Elvis near the end,
a giant in a soiled jumpsuit,
blank, useful for percentages,
a sheet from which the music's fled.

DAVID WILSON

The Glory

The glory of the beauty of the morning,
The cuckoo crying over the untouched dew;
The blackbird that has found it, and the dove
That tempts me on to something sweeter than love;
White clouds ranged even and fair as new-mown hay:
The heat, the stir, the sublime vacancy
Of sky and meadow and forest and my own heart:
The glory invites me, yet it leaves me scorning
All I can ever do, all I can be,
Beside the lovely of motion, shape, and hue,
The happiness I fancy fit to dwell
In beauty's presence. Shall I now this day
Begin to seek as far as heaven, as hell,
Wisdom or strength to match this beauty, start
And tread the pale dust pitted with small dark drops,
In hope to find whatever it is I seek,
Hearkening to short-lived happy-seeming things
That we know naught of, in the hazel copse?
Or must I be content with discontent
As larks and swallows are perhaps with wings?
And shall I ask at the day's end once more
What beauty is, and what I can have meant
By happiness? And shall I let all go,
Glad, weary, or both? Or shall I perhaps know
That I was happy oft and oft before,
Awhile forgetting how I am fast pent,
How dreary-swift, with naught to travel to,
Is Time? I cannot bite the day to the core.

EDWARD THOMAS

The Last One

Well they'd made up their minds to be everywhere because why not.
Everywhere was theirs because they thought so.
They with two leaves they whom the birds despise.
In the middle of stones they made up their minds.
They started to cut.

Well they cut everything because why not.
Everything was theirs because they thought so.
It fell into its shadow and they took both away.
Some to have some for burning.

Well cutting everything they came to the water.
They came to the end of the day there was one left standing.
They would cut it tomorrow they went away.
The night gathered in the last branches.
The shadow of the night gathered in the shadow on the water.
The night and the shadow put on the same head.
And it said Now.

Well in the morning they cut the last one.
Like the others the last one fell into its shadow.
It fell into its shadow on the water.
They took it away its shadow stayed on the water.
Well they shrugged they started trying to get the shadow away.
They cut right to the ground the shadow stayed whole.
They laid boards on it the shadow came out on top.

They shone lights on it the shadow got blacker and clearer.
They exploded the water the shadow rocked.
They built a huge fire on the roots.
They sent up black smoke between the shadow and the sun.
The new shadow flowed without changing the old one.
They shrugged they went away to get stones.

They came back the shadow was growing.
They started setting up stones it was growing.
They looked the other way it went on growing.
They decided they would make a stone out of it.
They took stones to the water they poured them into the shadow.
They poured them in they poured them in the stones vanished.
The shadow was not filled it went on growing.
That was one day.

The next day it was just the same it went on growing.
They did all the same things it was just the same.
They decided to take its water from under it.
They took away water they took it away the water went down.
The shadow stayed where it was before.
It went on growing it grew onto the land.
They started to scrape the shadow with machines.
When it touched the machines it stayed on them.
They started to beat the shadow with sticks.
Where it touched the sticks it stayed on them.
They started to beat the shadow with hands.
Where it touched the hands it stayed on them.
That was another day.

Well the next day started about the same it went on growing.
They pushed lights into the shadow.
Where the shadow got onto them they went out.
They began to stomp on the edge it got their feet.
And when it got their feet they fell down.
It got into eyes the eyes went blind.

The ones that fell down it grew over and they vanished.
The ones that went blind and walked into it vanished.
The ones that could see and stood still
It swallowed their shadows.
Then it swallowed them too and they vanished.
Well the others ran.

The ones that were left went away to live if it would let them.
They went as far as they could.
The lucky ones with their shadows.

W. S. MERWIN

#Extinction Rebellion

The day will come when papers
will only tell leaf-stories
of blackbirds' quarrels with sparrows.

Their pages will roll back into trees
and the front page will be bark.

Tabloids will be hundred-winged birds
singing earth anthems.

I'll settle into the buttress root of my armchair
and watch ants swarm

to text me secrets from the soil
adding emojis
of all our lost species.

I'll be surrounded by phones
that light up with chlorophyll,
vibrating like workers in their hives –

an apiary of apps.

I'll touch a vanda orchid
and it'll open
easily as hypertext,

everyone will hold leaves
intently as smartphones

to hear them retweet birdsong
from archives.

This is my homepage, where I belong.
This is my wood wide web,

my contour map
with which to navigate
a new internet –

rootlets sparkling towards rootlets
underground.

Underground
where resistance is in progress –

fungal friends working in darkness,
their windows blacked out.

PASCALE PETIT

Dust of Snow

The way a crow
Shook down on me
The dust of snow
From a hemlock tree

Has given my heart
A change of mood
And saved some part
Of a day I had rued.

ROBERT FROST

Water

The water understands
Civilization well;
It wets my foot, but prettily,
It chills my life, but wittily,
It is not disconcerted,
It is not broken-hearted:
Well used, it decketh joy,
Adorneth, doubleth joy:
Ill used, it will destroy,
In perfect time and measure
With a face of golden pleasure
Elegantly destroy.

RALPH WALDO EMERSON

Where Water Comes Together with Other Water

I love creeks and the music they make.
And rills, in glades and meadows, before
they have a chance to become creeks.
I may even love them best of all
for their secrecy. I almost forgot
to say something about the source!
Can anything be more wonderful than a spring?
But the big streams have my heart too.
And the places streams flow into rivers.
The open mouths of rivers where they join the sea.
The places where water comes together
with other water. Those places stand out
in my mind like holy places.
But these coastal rivers!
I love them the way some men love horses
or glamorous women. I have a thing
for this cold swift water.
Just looking at it makes my blood run
and my skin tingle. I could sit
and watch these rivers for hours.
Not one of them like any other.
I'm 45 years old today.
Would anyone believe it if I said
I was once 35?
My heart empty and sere at 35!
Five more years had to pass
before it began to flow again.
I'll take all the time I please this afternoon
before leaving my place alongside this river.
It pleases me, loving rivers.
Loving them all the way back
to their source.
Loving everything that increases me.

RAYMOND CARVER

Abstracted Water

Abstracted water, captive for a while,
becomes abstract, a proposition in hydraulics,

slops through lock-machines, goes level,
carries coal, parties, makes money,

slides back into Nature, used. If it hadn't come
leaking out of the hills to be cornered

you could synthesize it: a float-medium,
liquid vermiculite, a thin gel

flavoured with diesel,
rust, warm discharges.

The Cut's a notion, an idea cleaner than a river,
and closed at both ends. It's venture-water.

The design depth doesn't allow for motor-bikes, or
layers of sunken gondolas from supermarkets;

Garbage In, Garbage Out. The boat called 'Heritage'
comes dredging. Nothing much fronts

the canal. Where buildings on a street
stare you out, here it's you who do the looking,

left in your peace a little way
from the backside of it all, among

blank, patched-up walls with huge
secrets that stink and flare,

piss out coloured suds. Secrets
half-guarded, absorbed; secrets forgotten,

left to decay, bursting apart,
letting the dead stuff spill out. Sunlight

under bridges stays enclosed,
lattices to and fro. There's a law

dirt grows out of.

ROY FISHER

What the Clyde Said, After COP26

I keep the heid. I'm cool.
If asked – but you never ask –
I'd answer in tongues
hinting of linns, of Leven,
Nethan, Kelvin, Cart –
but neutral, balancing
both banks equally as I flow . . .

Do I judge? I mind the hammer-swing,
the welders' flash, the heavy
steel-built hulls I bore downstream
from my city, and maybe
I was a blether-skite then,
a wee bit full of myself,
when we seemed gey near unstoppable . . .

But how can I stomach any more
of these storm rains? How can I
slip quietly away to meet my lover,
the wide-armed Ocean, knowing
I'm a poisoned chalice
she must drain, drinking
everything you chuck away . . .

So these days I'm a listener, aye.
Think of me as a long level
liquid ear gliding slowly by.
I heard the world's words,
the pleas of peoples born
where my ships once sailed,
I heard the beautiful promises . . .

and, sure, I'm a river,
but I can take a side.
From this day, I'd rather keep afloat,
like wee folded paper boats,
the hopes of the young folk
chanting at my bank,
fear in their spring-bright eyes

so hear this:

fail them, and I will rise.

KATHLEEN JAMIE

catastrophic devastation; damage complete

Enough of rapid water.
Enough of the current and roar.
Enough of the anger. Enough of the Calder.
Enough of the Eden and Lune and the Cocker,
the Aire and the Derwent, the Ribble and Greta.
Enough of the Don and the Dee and the Culter.

Enough of the waiting. Enough of the checking.
Enough of waking up each night to listen
to rain, the rhythm of rain on the roof.
Enough of the grief, of packing your stuff.
Enough of slipping and losing your footing,
of trying to stand up again.

Enough of being wet, of water.
Enough of tap and bath and shower;
enough of gentle rain on flowers.
Enough of love and where it takes us –
ruined places. Enough of broken shops
and homes. Enough of dreams. Enough of plans.

Enough of made-up words for weather.
Enough of words that did not save us.
Enough of friends with shut-down faces.
Enough of toppled trees, uprooted;
enough of major structures shifted,
enough of wood and concrete lifted,

enough of nothing left
to lift, enough of nothing left.
Enough of loss. Enough of luck.
Enough of Whalley, Keswick, York.
Enough of what will not come back.
Enough of what we could not change.

Enough of grief and anger, love –
enough. Enough of rain.

CLARE SHAW

Letter to Noah's Wife

You are never mentioned on Ararat
or elsewhere, but I know a woman's hand
in salvation when I see it. Lately,
I'm torn between despair and ignorance.
I'm not a vegetarian, shop plastic,
use an air conditioner. Is this what happens
before it all goes fluvial? Do the selfish
grow self-conscious by the withering
begonias? Lately, I worry every black dress
will have to be worn to a funeral.
New York a bouillon, eroded filigree.
Anything but illness, I beg the plagues,
but shiny crows or nuclear rain.
Not a drop in London May through June.
I bask in the wilt by golden hour light.
Lately, only lately, it is late, tucking
our families into the safeties of the past.
My children, will they exist by the time
it's irreversible? Will they live
astonished at the thought of ice
not pulled from the mouth of a machine?
Which parent will be the one to break
the myth: the Arctic wasn't Sisyphus's
snowy hill. Noah's wife, I am wringing
my hands not knowing how to know
and move forward. Was it you
who gathered flowers once the earth
had dried? How did you explain the light
to all the animals?

MAYA C. POPA

Dover Beach

The sea is calm tonight.
The tide is full, the moon lies fair
Upon the straits; on the French coast the light
Gleams and is gone; the cliffs of England stand,
Glimmering and vast, out in the tranquil bay.
Come to the window, sweet is the night-air!
Only, from the long line of spray
Where the sea meets the moon-blanched land,
Listen! you hear the grating roar
Of pebbles which the waves draw back, and fling,
At their return, up the high strand,
Begin, and cease, and then again begin,
With tremulous cadence slow, and bring
The eternal note of sadness in.

Sophocles long ago
Heard it on the Aegean, and it brought
Into his mind the turbid ebb and flow
Of human misery; we
Find also in the sound a thought,
Hearing it by this distant northern sea.

The Sea of Faith
Was once, too, at the full, and round earth's shore
Lay like the folds of a bright girdle furled.
But now I only hear
Its melancholy, long, withdrawing roar,
Retreating, to the breath
Of the night-wind, down the vast edges drear
And naked shingles of the world.

Ah, love, let us be true
To one another! for the world, which seems
To lie before us like a land of dreams,
So various, so beautiful, so new,
Hath really neither joy, nor love, nor light,
Nor certitude, nor peace, nor help for pain;
And we are here as on a darkling plain
Swept with confused alarms of struggle and flight,
Where ignorant armies clash by night.

MATTHEW ARNOLD

Seascape

This celestial seascape, with white herons got up as angels,
flying as high as they want and as far as they want sidewise
in tiers and tiers of immaculate reflections;
the whole region, from the highest heron
down to the weightless mangrove island
with bright green leaves edged neatly with bird-droppings
like illumination in silver,
and down to the suggestively Gothic arches of the mangrove roots
and the beautiful pea-green back-pasture
where occasionally a fish jumps, like a wild-flower
in an ornamental spray of spray;
this cartoon by Raphael for a tapestry for a Pope:
it does look like heaven.
But a skeletal lighthouse standing there
in black and white clerical dress,
who lives on his nerves, thinks he knows better.
He thinks that hell rages below his iron feet,
that that is why the shallow water is so warm,
and he knows that heaven is not like this.
Heaven is not like flying or swimming,
but has something to do with blackness and a strong glare
and when it gets dark he will remember something
strongly worded to say on the subject.

ELIZABETH BISHOP

The Starlight Night

Look at the stars! look, look up at the skies!
  O look at all the fire-folk sitting in the air!
  The bright boroughs, the circle-citadels there!
Down in dim woods the diamond delves! the elves'-eyes!
The grey lawns cold where gold, where quickgold lies!
  Wind-beat whitebeam! airy abeles set on a flare!
  Flake-doves sent floating forth at a farmyard scare! –
Ah well! it is all a purchase, all is a prize.

Buy then! bid then! – What? – Prayer, patience, alms, vows.
Look, look: a May-mess, like on orchard boughs!
  Look! March-bloom, like on mealed-with-yellow sallows!
These are indeed the barn: withindoors house
The shocks. This piece-bright paling shuts the spouse
  Christ home. Christ and his mother and all his hallows.

GERARD MANLEY HOPKINS

Star Midnight

Isn't the sky wider, isn't the air
Steeper, the stars more preening,
Isn't the mind climbing stair by stair
And gradually winning
Advantage over earth, earning the clear
Precisest meaning?

Summer suggests this or its evenings do
When stars break through the warm
Darkness. The bare hand stretches out to strew
A bracelet from its arm
And the mind is sure that it has caught the true
Ultimate calm.

A moth flits by. A cat calls out. The intent
Moment is held. An hour
Pours out not in bell-notes but by the consent
Of purest thought. Say prayer
Or say this is a settled argument,
Say we are near

Knowing beyond discoveries with names
Or theories, but worldly-wise
In ways astonishing beyond our dreams
Yet here before our eyes.
I take a star down and the air still gleams
More in those skies.

ELIZABETH JENNINGS

Stars and Planets

Trees are cages for them: water hold its breath
To balance them without smudging on its delicate meniscus.
Children watch them playing in their heavenly playground;
Men use them to lug ships across oceans, through firths.

They seem so twinkle-still, but they never cease
Inventing new spaces and huge explosions
And migrating in mathematical tribes over
The steppes of space at their outrageous ease.

It's hard to think that the earth is one –
This poor sad bearer of wars and disasters
Rolls-Roycing round the sun with its load of gangsters,
Attended only by the loveless moon.

NORMAN MACCAIG

A Match with the Moon

Weary already, weary miles tonight
I walked for bed: and so, to get some ease,
I dogged the flying moon with similes.
And like a wisp she doubled on my sight
In ponds; and caught in tree-tops like a kite;
And in a globe of film all liquorish
Swam full-faced like a silly silver fish;
Last like a bubble shot the welkin's height
Where my road turned, and got behind me, and sent
My wizened shadow craning round at me,
And jeered, 'So, step the measure, – one two three!'
And if I faced on her, looked innocent,
But just at parting, halfway down a dell,
She kissed me for goodnight. So you'll not tell.

DANTE GABRIEL ROSSETTI

Parallax

the unbearable lightness of being no one
Slavoj Žižek

The moon lay silent on the sea
as on a polished shelf
rolling out and rolling out
its white path to the self

But while I stood illumined
like a man in his own book
I knew I was encircled by
the blindspot of its look

Because the long pole of my gaze
was all that made it turn
I was the only thing on earth
the moon could not discern

At such unearthly distance
we are better overheard.
The moon was in my mouth. It said
A million eyes. One word

for Michael Longley

DON PATERSON

Plunder

I have appropriated the windy twittering of aspen leaves
into language, stealing something from reality like a
silverness: drop-scapes of ice from peak sheers:

much of the rise in brooks over slow-rolled glacial stones:
the loop of reeds over the shallow's edge when birds
feed on the rafts of algae: I have taken right out of the

air the clear streaks of bird music and held them in my
head like shifts of sculpture glint: I have sent language
through the mud roils of a raccoon's paws like a net,

netting the roils: made my own uses of a downwind's
urgency on a downward stream: held with a large scape
of numbness the black distance upstream to the mountains

flashing and bursting: meanwhile, everything else, frog,
fish, bear, gnat has turned in its provinces and made off
with its uses: my mind's indicted by all I've taken.

A. R. AMMONS

Quartz

after Eeva Kilpi

As the light relaxes its hold
I will continue in the valley
to lather, like two chunks
of soap, quartz
between my palms,
while dim moths settle
on dim cushions
of campion.

The milky faces of the mineral
shear together, flint forth
claret sparks, like fireflies.

Don't tell me, if you know
how it happens.

JEN HADFIELD

Prayer

Here I work in the hollow of God's hand
with Time bent round into my reach. I touch
the circle of the earth, I throw and catch
the sun and moon by turns into my mind.
I sense the length of it from end to end,
I sway me gently in my flesh and each
point of the process changes as I watch;
the flowers come, the rain follows the wind.

And all I ask is this – and you can see
how far the soul, when it goes under flesh,
is not a soul, is small and creaturish –
that every day the sun comes silently
to set my hands to work and that the moon
turns and returns to meet me when it's done.

ALICE OSWALD

Postscript

And some time make the time to drive out west
Into County Clare, along the Flaggy Shore,
In September or October, when the wind
And the light are working off each other
So that the ocean on one side is wild
With foam and glitter, and inland among stones
The surface of a slate-grey lake is lit
By the earthed lightning of a flock of swans,
Their feathers roughed and ruffling, white on white,
Their fully grown headstrong-looking heads
Tucked or cresting or busy underwater.
Useless to think you'll park and capture it
More thoroughly. You are neither here nor there,
A hurry through which known and strange things pass
As big soft buffetings come at the car sideways
And catch the heart off guard and blow it open.

SEAMUS HEANEY

Your Choices Here

Acknowledgements

The publishers are grateful to the following for permission to reproduce copyright material.

Fleur Adcock, 'The Spirit of the Place', from *Collected Poems* (Bloodaxe Books, 2024).

Jason Allen-Paisant, 'Daffodils', from *Thinking with Trees* (Carcanet, 2021).

A. R. Ammons, 'Plunder', from *Selected Poems*. Copyright © 1986 by A. R. Ammons, from *Selected Poems* 1986 by A. R. Ammons. Used by permission of W. W. Norton & Company, Inc.

Simon Armitage, 'I Kicked a Mushroom', from *The Unaccompanied* by Simon Armitage (Faber and Faber Limited).

Simon Armitage, 'The Summit', from *The Cryosphere* (Faber and Faber Limited).

Elizabeth Bishop, 'The Moose' and 'Seascape', from *Poems: the Centenary Edition* (Chatto & Windus, 2011), copyright © Elizabeth Bishop, 2011. Reprinted by permission of the Random House Group Limited.

Eavan Boland, 'The Blossom', from *New Collected Poems* (Carcanet Press, 2005).

Sean Borodale, '3rd July: Gift', from *Bee Journal* by Sean Borodale published by Jonathan Cape. Copyright © Sean Borodale, 2012. Reprinted by permission of The Random House Group Limited.

Jean Binta Breeze, 'earth cries', from *Third World Girl: Selected poems, with Live DVD* (Bloodaxe Books, 2011).

Robert Bringhurst, 'A Lesson in Botany' and 'Anecdote of the Squid', from *Selected Poems* by Robert Bringhurst published by Jonathan Cape. Copyright © Robert Bringhurst, 2010. Reprinted by permission of The Random House Group Limited.

John Burnside, 'Peregrines', from *All One Breath* by John Burnside published by Jonathan Cape. Copyright © John Burnside, 2014. Reprinted by permission of The Random House Group Limited.

Raymond Carver, 'Where Water Comes Together with Other Water', from *All of Us: The Collected Poems* (The Harvill Press, 1996). Copyright © Tess Gallagher. Reproduced by permission of The Wylie Agency, 250 West 57th Street, Suite 2114, New York, NY 10107.

Gillian Clarke, 'Neighbours', from *Letting in the Rumour* (Fyfield Books, 1991). Reproduced by permission of the author c/o Rogers, Coleridge & White, 20 Powis Mews, London W11 1JN.

Lucille Clifton, 'the earth is a living thing' and 'surely I am able to write poems' and 'the beginning of the end of the world', from *The Collected Poems of Lucille Clifton 1965–2010* (BOA Editions, 2012).

Dennis Craig, 'Flowers', from *West Indian Poetry: An anthology for schools* (Longman Caribbean, 1971), copyright © Longman Group Limited.

e e cummings, '(O sweet spontaneous)', from *Complete Poems 1904–1962* (Liveright, 1991). Reproduced by permission of W. W. Norton & Co.

Tjawangwa Dema, 'Black Bear in the Grocery Store', from *an/other pastoral* (No Bindings, 2022).

Imtiaz Dharker, 'The Host', from *Shadow Reader* (Bloodaxe Books, 2024).

Emily Dickinson, 'A Narrow Fellow in the Grass', from *Emily Dickinson's Poems: As She Preserved Them* (Harvard University Press, 2016), copyright © The President and Fellows of Harvard College 2016.

Carol Ann Duffy, 'Parliament', from *The Bees* (Picador, 2011), copyright © Carol Ann Duffy 2011.

Paul Farley, 'For the House Sparrow, In Decline', from *The Ice Age* (Picador, 2002), © Paul Farley 2002.

Vicki Feaver, 'Eagle Owl', from *The Book of Blood* by Vicki Feaver, published by Jonathan Cape. Copyright © Vicki Feaver, 2006. Reprinted by permission of The Random House Group Limited.

Roy Fisher, 'Abstracted Water', from *Abstracted Water* (Oxford University Press, 1994).

Isabel Galleymore, 'The Starfish', from *Significant Other* (Carcanet Press, 2019).

John Glenday, 'The Walkers', from *The Golden Mean* (Picador, 2015), copyright © John Glenday 2015.

Louise Glück, 'Daisies', from *The Wild Iris* (Carcanet Press, 1996).

Jorie Graham, 'Poem', from *Runaway* (Carcanet Press, 2020).

Jen Hadfield, 'Quartz', from *Byssus* (Picador, 2014), copyright © Jen Hadfield 2014.

Seamus Heaney, 'Postscript', from *The Spirit Level* by Seamus Heaney (Faber and Faber Limited).

Seamus Heaney, 'Song', from *Field Work* by Seamus Heaney (Faber and Faber Limited).

Sean Hewitt, 'Dryad', from *Tongues of Fire* by Sean Hewitt published by Jonathan Cape. Copyright © Sean Hewitt, 2020. Reprinted by permission of The Random House Group Limited.

Matthew Hollis, 'The Blackbird of Spitalfields', from *Earth House* (Bloodaxe Books, 2023).

Kathleen Jamie, 'Wings Over Scotland', from *The Bonniest Companie* (Picador, 2015), copyright © Kathleen Jamie 2015.

Kathleen Jamie, 'What the Clyde said, after COP26', copyright © Kathleen Jamie 2021. Reproduced by kind permission of the author.

Elizabeth Jennings, 'Star Midnight', from *Consequently I Rejoice* (Carcanet Press, 1977).

Patrick Kavanagh, 'Innocence', from *Collected Poems* by Patrick Kavanagh, published by Allen Lane. Copyright © Patrick Kavanagh, 2004. Reprinted by permission of The Random House Group Limited.

Zaffar Kunial, 'Hawthorn', from *England's Green* by Zaffar Kunial (Faber and Faber Limited). Reproduced by kind permission of the author.

Theophilus Kwek, '24.6.16 Red Kites', from *The First Five Storms* (Smith Doorstop Books, 2017).

Denise Levertov, 'In California: Morning, Evening, Late January', from *A Door in the Hive / Evening Train* (Bloodaxe Books, 1993).

Frances Leviston, 'Unbeliever', copyright © Frances Leviston 2024. Reproduced by kind permission of the author.

Norman MacCaig, 'Basking Shark', from *The Many Days: Selected Poems of Norman MacCaig* (Birlinn Ltd, 2022). Reproduced with permission of the Licensor through PLSclear.

Norman MacCaig, 'Toad' and 'Stars and Planets', from *The Many Days: Selected Poems of Norman MacCaig* (Birlinn Ltd, 2022). Reproduced with permission of the Licensor through PLSclear.

Jess McKinney, 'The Deer', first appeared in *Weeding* by Jess McKinney, published in 2021 by Hazel Press. Reproduced by kind permission of the author.

Louis MacNeice, 'Snow', from *The Collected Poems of Louis MacNeice* (Faber and Faber Limited). © Estate of Louis MacNeice, reprinted by permission of David Higham Associates.

Paula Meehan, 'Death of a Field', from *Painting Rain* (Carcanet Press, 2009).

W. S. Merwin, 'The Last One', from *The Lice* (Atheneum, 1974). Copyright © W. S. Merwin. Reproduced by permission of The Wylie Agency, 250 West 57th Street, Suite 2114, New York, NY 10107.

Edwin Muir, 'The Late Wasp', from *Collected Poems* by Edwin Muir (Faber and Faber Limited).

Paul Muldoon, 'Hedgehog', from *New Weather* (Faber and Faber Limited).

Les Murray, 'Pigs' and 'from "Walking to the Cattle Place"', from *New Collected Poems* (Carcanet Press, 2003).

Frank O'Hara, 'The Hunter', from *Selected Poems* (Carcanet Press, 1998).

Mary Oliver, 'Fox', from *West Wind* (Houghton Mifflin Harcourt, 1997).

Alice Oswald, 'Walking Past a Rose This June Morning' and 'Prayer', from *Woods etc.* (Faber and Faber Limited).

Mark Pajak, 'Brood', from *Slide* by Mark Pajak published by Jonathan Cape. Copyright © Mark Pajak, 2022. Reprinted by permission of The Random House Group Limited.

Don Paterson, 'Parallax', from *Rain*. Published by Faber & Faber. Copyright © Don Paterson. Reproduced by permission of the author c/o Rogers, Coleridge & White, 20 Powis Mews, London W11 1JN.

Pascale Petit, '#Extinction Rebellion', from *Tiger Girl* (Bloodaxe Books, 2020).

Ruth Pitter, 'Leafcutter Bees', from *Poems 1926-1966* published by The Cresset Press/Barrie & Rockcliff). Copyright © Ruth Pitter, 1968. Reprinted by permission of The Random House Group Limited.

Maya C. Popa, 'Letter to Noah's Wife', from *Wound is the Origin of Wonder* (Picador, 2023), copyright © Maya C. Popa 2023.

Stephanie Pruitt, 'Mississippi Gardens', reprinted by permission of Stephanie Pruitt.

Kathleen Raine, 'Heirloom', from *Collected Poems* (Golgonooza Press, 2000).

Roger Robinson, 'Midwinter', from *A Portable Paradise* (Peepal Tree Press, 2019).

Theodore Roethke, 'Moss-Gathering', from *Collected Poems* (Faber and Faber Limited).

Carl Sandburg, 'Grass', from *Cornhuskers* (Henry Holt & Co., 1918), copyright © Carl Sandburg. Reproduced by permission of Macmillan.

Olive Senior, 'Pineapple', from *Gardening in the Tropics* (Bloodaxe Books, 1995).

Jo Shapcott, 'The Mad Cow Believes She Is the Spirit of the Weather', from *Phrase Book* (Oxford University Press, 1992). Reproduced by permission of Georgina Capel Associates Limited.

Clare Shaw, 'catastrophic devastation; damage complete', from *Flood* (Bloodaxe Books, 2018).

C. H. Sisson, 'The Red Admiral', from *Collected Poems* (Carcanet Press, 1998).

Stevie Smith, 'Alone in the Woods' and 'The Donkey', from *The Collected Poems and Drawings of Stevie Smith* (Faber and Faber Limited).

Karen Solie, 'Mole', from *The Road In Is Not the Same Road Out* (Farrar, Straus & Giroux, 2015). Reproduced by permission of the author c/o Rogers, Coleridge & White, 20 Powis Mews, London W11 1JN.

A. E. Stallings, 'Explaining an Affinity for Bats', from *Hapax* (TriQuarterly Books/Northwestern University Press, 2006), copyright © A. E. Stallings 2006.

Wallace Stevens, 'The Snow Man', from *Collected Poems* by Wallace Stevens (Faber and Faber Limited).

Anne Stevenson, 'Swifts', from *Collected Poems* (Bloodaxe Books, 2023).

Katharine Towers, 'Iceberg Season', from *The Remedies* (Picador, 2016), copyright © Katharine Towers 2016.

David Wilson, 'Everest', from *The Equilibrium Line* (Smith Doorstop Books, 2019).